More Advance Praise for White Boots

"To the list of great poets whose names are synonymous with the places they describe—Stafford's Northwest, Frost's New England, Levine's Detroit, Charles Wright's Appalachia—you can now add William Pitt Root's *White Boots: New and Selected Poems of West.* These poems of tender awe and Rilkean praise, erasing completely the divisions between man and beast, invite the reader upon their backs to be carried across buttes and vistas, arroyos and sheer cliff shimmy holes; the music is wound so tight that stitches and sinews disappear. All that remains is the pure imagination made manifest and majestic, the reader alone riding their shine." —**KEITH FLYNN**

"William Pitt Root's magnificent *White Boots: New and Selected Poems of the West* creates an essential epic journey of a 'heart familiar with disaster,' a journey that takes us from the earth itself, even underground and all that is held there, history, myth, the work and dreams of generations, in order 'to call down upon earth/ a whole sky full of stars,/ the entire firmament of fire.' The people and landscape of the west, in stunning stories and images of earth, sky, light, darkness—that is, the essential elements that surround us—are held together in a voice whose sublime art is also its invaluable humanity. Ending with images of floating, of an earth redefined by experiences it holds, it is fitting that the book closes with a kind of coda: his wolf dog enters and becomes part of the work itself, the natural world entering the world of art. For Root, the world is a poem; for us, his is a world we need to enter."
—**RICHARD JACKSON**

White Boots
New and Selected Poems of the West

William Pitt Root

[signature: Wm Pitt Root]

Poetry Series #8

CAROLINA WREN PRESS
Durham, North Carolina

The mission of Carolina Wren Press is to seek out, nurture, and promote literary work by new and underrepresented writers, including women and writers of color.

Editor: Andrea Selch

Design: Lesley Landis Designs
Cover Image: "White Boots" © 1988 James G. Davis

Library of Congress Cataloguing-in-Publication Data

Root, William Pitt, 1941-
White boots: new & selected poems of the West / William Pitt Root.
p. cm. -- (Carolina Wren Press poetry series ; 8)
ISBN 0-932112-51-X
I. Title.

PS3568.O66W48 2006
811'.54--dc22

2006016711

Acknowledgements

I once again thank my vivacious wife and tireless partner, Pamela Uschuk, herself one of the best, most impassioned poets this country has produced.

Of course the author also wishes to thank Andrea Selch for her patience and help in shepherding this manuscript into print and James G. Davis for his generosity in permitting the use one of his works as the cover art.

And finally, I acknowledge each of the utterly indispensable cadre of animal companions who helped keep our various households loving and lively throughout the duration: Grizzly, Mu, CyCluppy, Oscar "de Leon" Wild, Drambuie, Lulu, Maxine, Sheba, Happy, and Sadie.

And I would like also to thank, respectively and respectfully, Keith Browning, the late Harry Ford, Ed Ochester, and Jim Hepworth, for previously collecting a number of these poems in *Coot and Other Characters* (1977), *Invisible Guests* (1981), *Reasons For Going It On Foot* (1981), *Faultdancing* (1986), and *Trace Elements from a Recurring Kingdom* (1994). The author also wishes to thank Ray Gonzales, editor of Mesilla Press, for having first published "The Well of Twilight" in his pamphlet series.

The author wishes to thank the editors of the following magazines and anthologies in which most of these works originally appeared: *The Atlantic Monthly; Bark; Columbia: A Magazine of Prose and Poetry; Comeback Wolves: Western Writers Welcome the Wolf Home; Crossing the River: Poets of the American West, High Plains Quarterly, The Lucid Stone; Many Mountains Moving; The Morrow Anthology of Younger American Poets; OnEarth, Olive Tree Review; Only Morning in Her Shoes: Poems about Women Aging; Poetry; Quarterly West; SouthEast Arts Journal* [England]; *Southwest: A Contemporary Anthology; The Tuscon Poet; Turnrow; Unplugged Guttenberg; Where Are We: The Montana Poets Anthology; Wildwood Review.*

"Out There" first appeared in *The Atlantic Monthly;* "Craft" first appeared in *Poetry* (Chicago).

WHITE BOOTS:
GHOST OF THE SAN MANUEL MINE
for James G. Davis

As you know, Jim, I did work underground
in the same mine you've imagined
    in your studio: half a mile down, taking
wages enough to make it to California
and fool's gold enough to remind me
    I don't know much after all.

New guys like myself—still thrilled
by the dangers of fire or falling
    through the dark into a hole followed
by twenty tons of dusty rumbling ore—,
we all tried to stay alert
    each minute of the eight-hour shift.

And for a week or two, alert we were,
then habit made us careless as the rest
    so we'd pocket our safety glasses,
let dust masks dangle from our necks
and sometimes catch each other
    stepping out across open shafts

without first snapping our lanyards
to the rusty cables overhead.
    The buddy system wasn't much observed,
so like the rest come break time
I'd kick back alone against the stone wall
    and light up, flicking my headlamp off

so the dark expanded, flooding gently
through my eyes. In the distance,
    sometimes, a solitary hunched figure
projecting its small wedge of light
would glide by my line's entrance
    tiny as a fly in a tear of amber

from where I watched, invisible
and isolate as a stone in outer space,
        or inner space. Just some guy.

Never saw old White Boots in those days
but often thought how all those men
        just lost in the Sunshine Mine
must have felt—poor bastards
who lived long enough to feel,
        long enough to lose everything
in their minds but hope
before their air was gone, long after
        their light. You'd have to kill your light

to keep from igniting whatever gasses
might be seeping from walls,
        so dark is where you'd be,
whether by yourself or in the company of others.
In such a dark I had no need of White Boots, my friend,
        but looking at this image, startling, almost comic,

you've drawn from the dark of blinding inks
and your own heart familiar with disaster,
        I'm reminded now of how it is
the living keep hold of the things
that bind them to those gone—
        how gypsies, when a loved one's dying,

will help the one failing stay just a little longer
by turning a wooden chair upsidedown
        to hold between them. On one leg
a live hand, the dying on another,
until, ready, it falls free. But
        the thing is the clasp itself

across that final distance,
how it allows those last things
    that need saying to be said.
That's how it's always seemed
to me, with art I mean. Whether
    it's paint on canvas or ink on a page,

it's the chance for what knows it must die in us
to join what knows it will live forever.
    And knowledge from such a common depth
only survives in the light as shadow,
as White Boots, *imago*, as a way, meanwhile,
    to stay in touch while the sun burns on.

OLD HAND

After a few days underground
without any of us panicking
and falling down a killer shaft,
they figure we might last so
we're turned over to an old-timer
whose boulder of a body
hunches round the double-jack
he shows us how to wield. His
hair's the wild worn silver
of the hammerhead in his hand.
He finds us, at best, amusing
and has each of the three of us
take a couple whacks at rocks
which chip but do not sunder.
Us with our young muscles,
him with his crooked look.
Then he takes the double-jack,
taps the biggest rock once
and swings cutting it clean.
We all look at each other,
shaking our heads, chagrined.
It's pure defeat. "Thing's this,"
he says, aside. "Rock knows
where the cracks are
so you ask rock, politely.
Tap gentle-like, like this,
it maps out fracture-lines. Tap,
watch the dust shift then just
where it shows you to strike
strike." Easier said than done. But
that's one lesson I never forgot,
that and the crooked grin
made of an old man's iron.

ANAMAX OPEN PIT: Graveyard Shift
    for Patti MacGill

1.
Even with her engine blasting
    and the lowered scraper blade pressing
tons of rubble through the dark,
    this much is clear: As far as she can see

submarine light of a full green winter moon
    inundates this desert
shimmering like the ocean which shifted here millions of years
    before these mountains rose.

        Fossils lie like bookmarks
     pressed among pages of stone
reciting vivid memories of the sea into the air.

        Mount Lemmon, sacred
       to the first people here,
looms brooding above the murk like a monstrous omen

    from the dream no headlight
    can expose, no blade force.
Yet the bright arc of her blade does force

        mound upon mound of ore
     as her headlights catch the tips
of distant saguaros, rising alert as totems from the desert floor.

2.
    She cuts the engine
then the lights
    and waits. Dust
falls from overhead, Orion
    brightens. Desert in

the dark grows luminous,
    as in another corner
of the pit shovels and dozers
    groan and roar like
huge abyssal creatures
    feeding in the circles
of their own light.

The great tire
    she leans against
for warmth is
    as if alive, hot,
ridged, dusty skin
    almost reptilian.
The first bitter breath
    of coffee rises
from her steel thermos
    and slowly, after hours
of headlights leaching
    color from the rocks,
she sees again
    the slate blue moonlit
shades of hills and sky,
    orange and yellow glints
of stars, red, blue,
    aqueous wavering green.

3.
The meteoric flare, shock-white,
falls so close
she hears it hiss

as all around her
by that instant light

is shown—ruinous geometric
wound of the pit,
saguaros at the rim
stationed like sentinels—

before waters of darkness
engulf her startled face,
extinguish the live glow of her hands.

4.
In that newly declared dark,
from some neighboring ravine
no blade has yet torn apart,
a spectral band of coyotes start
as if to call down upon earth
a whole sky full of stars,
the entire firmament of fire,
crying out their cries like prayers
to the ear of Time, which listens
through one woman, who hears.

AT THE FOOT OF A HOLY MOUNTAIN

Nothing seems more still
than this desert at night,
late, after the breezes
of twilight
establish themselves
in the chaparral.

The crickets are quiet
and the moon is silent
as a sailboat
in a children's book
here where each incarnate scrap
hunts for another,
cold glass eyes
fired by night hunger.

Webbed feet and scaled bellies
scour the rocks and sand
while wings overhead
cross and recross
the scarred face of the moon
and all the idiots of appetite
pursue each other blindly
by the jeweled light of their jeweled eyes.

IN THE TALL WELL OF TWILIGHT
for Andy, Chuck, Bruce

And there we hunkered sweaty as toads in the tall well of twilight
three men wrapping up a day in the sun
grunting and stretching when *Look*
you said
toward the barn looming at the corner of
our eyes and the drainpipe upright
in the shadows *Look*
your voice tight in our throats now
and there it was
bullsnake on the drainpipe
quartz eyes expressionless
wide jaws a nest in which a baby pigeon fat and bald
sat imperially blinking
for all the world like an infant out in a stroller
or an admiral taking the deck
Sunday in the park
as the long throat below
sucked patiently pulsing like a cold wrist

Let's save it one of us started as we all sat staring
our arms and faces still locked in their
postures of release *Too late now*
way too late but look
at that innocence will you look at that
not a care in the world
and we looked all right and it looked around at us
head slowly sinking
bright eyes still unquestioning at the rim
and soon we all stirred restlessly and left the place
each one of us
blinking our way blindly into the dark coming on

LEARNING PRAYER AMONG STONES

To speak to rock
is to become rock,
whose mouth
is the gradual utterance
of sand
upon tongues of water
and the wind.
Is to be blind
to the nightvoid
and dayvoid
of moon and sun.
Reflections, origin:
Eyes of the owl
deep in saguaro
in the ghost of a sea,
eyes of the iguana
set in the sparkle
of the living surf.
Deaf. Numb to the cleavages
and crumbling of self.
To not speak.
To remain
among stones
a stone.

MAKING WAY

I was edgy, pulling out of a parking lot
into Tucson rush-hour traffic in Frog,
my old green Cougar with its skyroof wide,
my faithful 90-pound Oscar's head beside mine,
when I noticed the teenager noticing us
and nudging his buddies in the red pickup,
all of them craning around to see
the bearded guy and his dog, and just then
Oscar sneezed his magnificent flailing firehose
sneeze that covers a 180 degree arc nicely,
my face at about 160.
                       Off flew my glasses,
and as I wiped his high-velocity slobber
from cheek and forehead, those kids—maybe Apache,
maybe Pima or Tohono O'odham, all smiling like
brown Buddhas—left room for me to pull in.

How could I ever forget the joy in their smiles
at seeing this anglo-honkie get it from his dog
like that, how their broad gentle faces widened
with amusement, how their dark eyes glowed?
And how could I ever even begin to feel outrage
at unmannered Oscar, whose cousin after all
is old man Coyote—rule-breaker without equal,
who even at the peak of rush-hour traffic is alive and well,
whose tail is still wagging at the beginning of the 21st Century?

DESIGN THAT HAPPENS AS THE WORLD HAPPENS
in memory of my mother, Bonita

Even you can't count the winter hours of clouds and changing light
you sat, needles clicking
        as the bright coins of sun and moon
skipped across all the lakes and streams between us,
arcing in their course obscure as only daily acts can be.

Nor can I know just what wide net of dreams and recollections
may've opened in that heart of yours
while Northwest thunderheads slowly rubbed above you,
        wet sheep in their pasture of grey sky.
Working skein after skein of cocoa and ivory
softer than the fingers
each inch was drawn through, tenderly, firmly,
        you sat, all your unconscious care
divided up among daughters, cats, and absent son
milling in and out of the doors of love
and hunger, each requiring
        a flash of full attention
though your fingers would still flicker
through the half-light in your lap
        even as your kitten
found that the soft ball bright at your feet
could be made to skitter like a mouse
through the gamescape of its tiny skull.

Now, five states away from you, I remember on the desert
the adobe dwelling of a Navajo weaver
where I learned—as she shot the wooden shuttle *clack clack*
to lock each thread—that the design in every blanket
happens as the world happens:

This lightning
is the storm
that made me bring the loom
inside, these blue lines
are the rivers
fed by rain and here
the sun opened his eye again
and made the yellow wool
cry for its place
in this dream. Things
that happen: Catch them
in a blanket to keep you warm
when you remember
how it was before this time.

And so I do remember
because
I wear this sweater, this history
of the heart
shockingly tender as the laying on of hands.

Oracle, Arizona

CROSSING THE REZ
for Joy

I was hitching a ride toward twilight
southeast of Billings, middle of November,
when a pickup let me toss my gear in back.
I climbed up into the cab boozy with two old boys,
Country Western AM blaring sad songs of love.
The driver's sidekick cackled "Cold enough out there
to chrome a bobcat's balls." He hoisted a pint
of Jack, black, shoved it into my chapped hands.
It nearly thawed my tongue as they both jawboned
down the road, pointing out into uniform blue dark
toward Custer's Last Stand. "Never trust no Injun,
bud, don't matter *how* cold it gits," they soberly
advised, shaking their heads and slowing down,
dropping me off there smack on the Rez at sunset.

And there I stood the best part of a bad hour
until along came the first car that stopped,
a rumpled one-eyed station wagon, front bumper
dangling, muffler skidding ice-glazed blacktop
just like a kid's sparkler in the dark.
                              "Hop in, par'ner,"
and in I hopped, stiff with cold, duffle on my lap,
all the wide dark faces, in front and back,
flat and friendly as old Hank Williams
carried on about good love gone bad again
from a scratchy speaker loose on the dash.
One popped the top on a Bud for me as gradually
we picked up speed, tranny wailing like a wolf,
everybody howling themselves into Hank's fix,
off-key and flat, while we hurtled through
the dark in a one-eyed comet.

                        "Where you headed?"
I answered "Sheridan." He nodded, smiled.
"Thing is, enit, par'ner, we can't take you there.
Off-rez cops, they catch us in this heap,
hey, it's bail-time in the Rockies. When
we drop you at Wyola, just
remember this: Cold as your ass gets
don't park it in no cowboy pickup,
you'll do just fine. And do say howdy
for us In'dins to all the pretty girls
you meet on down the line."

TEACHING AMONG THE CHILDREN
OF CHIEF PLENTY COUPS

Late October and in this country
the dry gold of the leaves
falls like old ornaments.
A Christmas that hasn't come
feels done with. Branches
reach into the air like roots,
and whatever blossoms
blossoms underground. Here
most faces are flat as the earth
and colors of the earth, and when their speech
erupts with Crow earth fills the air
as words the stomach somehow hears.

Speak, and you will be heard.
But question one of them
expecting what you would expect
of stone, or an old stump,
the wide blank gaze, neither
friendly nor hostile,
of a flat rock, or bark
with eyes. It is not
a gaze that isolates
a tree from its forest
or mistakes
words from the tongue
for the heart's talk.

What you want to know here
you must learn here
from that open book
whose quick words burn
on pages shed like leaves
in gusts of sunlight. And remember
that no leaf is the tree,
no tree the land; nor would

the land itself explain the curved
blue shield of sky, the wheel
of the seasons turning, returning,
or the people who move freely still
among them all, alert
to the one wind moving
antelope and elk, eagle and owl
among their brothers
in the ritual of hunger, the hunters.

Pryor, Crow Reservation

SWEAT

I.
When I turn my headlights off, the night comes on
of cows in fields, their eyes
that gave our light back
gone now: Lumps
of darkness in the dark
crunching pebbles
under tall grass.

        A door
widens to lamplight, the dim faces
of strangers, brothers,
and the scent of smoke. On the walls
hides are hung—a small bear
with a hole between the ears,
two deer. From a raw post
in the center of the room,
mothlike brilliance shines
from the fanned tails
of three wild grouse.

Round stones heat
outside in a shallow pit
while we talk by the woodstove.
A hound in the far corner
snores as we strip.

II.
Into the dome through the hole
closing behind us: heat, dark,
only the glowing of the stones
as our bodies open to the heated air
that sizzles blindly up

into our faces. The scalding
presence of a handful of sage
torn from the cows' field
fills the dissolving universe.
Not me now, not you,
just darkness and the heat, a few words
from nowhere. Then nothing
but darkness, heat.
                    The entire
skin sobs with torture, pleasure
in the sizzle of steam,
the sear of sage. Darkness. Heat.
Skin has melted and muscles
soften like doeskin. Bones
surrender their rigidity and brain
gives up ideas as easily as lungs
give up the air or flesh its water,
spirit its tent of flesh.

III.
Out of the sweat lodge
of bowed willow sealed by hides
and darkness sealed in darkness,
we rush into the still water
charged by stars and frost:
Bodies slam shut, scream,
duck and cry out
cries of ice, of fire.

Stars on their dark axles turn,
blood in its old bloodbed
rushes, floods. The cows of darkness
move toward us now

as toward a newborn calf
still glistening in the grass.

We stand up in the night,
shivering, grinning,
silent among mountainous echoes
of our helplessness
as we dunk again.

We shine, and the world
everywhere around us
gives us back
our shining.

"DO YOU KNOW THE COUNTRY AROUND HERE"

My people are like
deer
more than people.
My mother's aunt told me
this
just after I was born.
The first time.

She told me
she was 13 and—do you
know the country
around here?—her
mother
was at Sacramento,
called that now,
when the white man came there
a hundred years ago
or more
and chased them,
killing all the men
and raping
women they could catch.
The old and sick
and young.
The men died once,
the women
every time. The women
lived.
        She was
13 then
and she hid under the leaves
and they came to Booneville,
they call it Booneville now,

and got away
and she didn't have to
hide in the leaves anymore then.

Our people are different.
My people are like the deer.
Nomads. They don't
settle like your people.
It was inevitable.
Your people were smarter.
Don't you think it was
inevitable? I can see it
in your eyes,
the way you are looking
at me now.

No, no, it's true.

Your eyes show me.

My people are like the deer.

Healdsburg, California

EXPLORING ONEONTA GORGE

Eyes bright as
backlit leaves,

here old gods
waded the gorge,

their deeply packed tracks
breaking into stones.

Balancing upon them
we walk on in

where no paths lead,
deeper and deeper,

each step
an unwitting prayer

to those we fail
to recognize gazing

back up at us
through the water's face.

Those before us,
those within,

those underfoot.

REASONS FOR GOING IT ON FOOT

I speed along knowing
the true journey

is on foot, hungry
and broke, learning

hour by hour local nuances
of accent and gesture

by which I may identify
myself as a stranger

eager to know
the ways of those

I beg my life from
as I pass.

LIGHT IN A HOUSE OF MIRRORS
Considerations at La Push

Island high as our inland hills
—John Logan

1.

I sleep in a clump of dark humped trees
where the river forks and roars below a bridge.

I sleep fitful as light in a house of mirrors,
dream of a drunken Indian
who sells me my own scalp slick as a skinned cat, dripping.

But when I wake and write to a friend
the dream I tell for her
is of a shape like my shape by the river,
filling slowly with sunlight
bright as honey, quick as rain.
A tall attentive glow beside dark water.

2.

Here were the flatfaced people whose earthfathers
circled toward
this land over a blue idea
of godliness
melting behind them, burning before.

3.

The flatfaced stones beneath my feet
predate Cezanne
longer than 10,000 redwoods end-to-end have lived
swallowing air and sunlight, rain and drifting
soil up into that gradual dance of the self
in whose shadow even long-lived tortoise withers—

Split and fracture,
      dark falls of light
squaring edges of the once-round stone.

Scald and freeze of passion's glance and intellect's regard.

4.
A great ghoul grey from the ruin of a log
rose like mist before me
as I took my last steps back to camp, startling
as if to distract me from my story.
                                        But no,
it was only my imagination, yellow-eyed and moss-faced
again.

5.
Once there was more land, higher than now. The waters grew jeal-
ous, gathered their tribes and conspired. Men knew this and the
greatest planned to flee inland, leaving the others—the sickly and
the weak—to form a wall to hold back the waters. So there they
stood, the abandoned, and the waters were indeed delayed before
they rushed inland. Today we can see the heads of the old ones at
the shore here, vast, moss-haired, silent. These were the runts, the
least of their race. And we feel dwarfed beside them. For the great-
fathers, who saved themselves, shrank among the safe places far
inland. At the edges of the waters those old stunted heroes still
stand guard. We call them stones so we will not remember. They
no longer speak to us, who are neither their sons nor daughters.

CRAFT

Back at the rectangular harbor
sheltered by its groins of stone,
mist, I knew, still would be rising
from spaces left by fishing boats
well before dawn, as this was
the annual one-day Halibut season
when men made or lost a fortune,
but just a hundred yards inland
among the looming Sitka Spruce
older than their namesake by
many centuries, there was sunlight
on the wood-carver's shoulder
and starlight in his voice.
He chanted one of the songs
of his people, over and over
under his breath. A song
for carving totems—for Wolf
and Raven, Eagle, Salmon—
a song for the carver carving.
The place was a native museum
where the carver wore jeans and
a flannel shirt, even a watch
"so I'll know when to break."
He answered several questions
during the casual half hour
before I asked if he ever tired
of carving the same traditional
totem over and over, if ever
he thought of starting one new.
The smell of cedar rose from
his blade, he smiled, the adze
raised a few more curls. "One day

a new dreamer will come among
the People—there will be fish
again, and game, and new stories
to show us once more a path
of light through the darkness.
Then, yes, there will be new totems.
Meanwhile," he said, resuming
his task, "we tread water,
we keep our tools sharp."

DEAR JEFFERS
A Note From Sheridan To Carmel-By-The-Sea

It's a long way from the queer remote silence-making quawk
of that heron your words snagged on the wing
as I was being born, Jeffers, decades ago,
in a Minnesota blizzard, and you were in a squall of rage
near Big Sur in the place no longer your place—
  as you forsaw, dragging stone after stone
to your tower nonetheless
from the live surf and froth of your own sweat.

Edged in now
by homes No-Man built to live in—high priced suckertraps
for those successful in that coming world you shunned and decried
poem after bitter poem—your stone tower, Jeffers,
                even your stone tower
raised by hand toward the high blue home
of those beloved hawks
toward whom you turned and turned your falcon of a face
        for evidence of worthiness,
is gone into their hands, their pockets,
enhanced by your famous hatred, the prices rising
with your skydriven fistlike poems exactly abhorring them.

Where I am, in Wyoming still magnificent with wilderness
no sea has breathed on for millions of years,
        the old forces
finding a new grip soon will ream out
ranchers and farmers bewildered by profits sudden as true
        strokes, making way for holes
into which men hungry for the good life
        will descend, innocent

of your hawks, gulls, godlike stallions, and women
with wild eyes will tend them
as some die, most prosper
       in the ways men do these days, surrounded
by the crown jewels of the age—
    appliances and gadgets designed to make
life careless. And they work, dear Jeffers. They do work.

OUT THERE
for Charles Levendosky

Wind like a razor
slides over the smooth
cheeks of the plains.

In my car I feel conspicuous.

I stop to walk
and turn to watch
the road laid like a
frown of stone across
the endlessness of grass.
The idling car is fatally apparent.

No map I carry hints at this.

Later, driving on,
I wonder what it is
out there that notices
me as I pass,
what sensibility thrives
in all that terrible vigilance of grass.

IN A PLACE SO EMPTY HOLLOW BONES ARE
THE ONLY HALLELUJAHS
for Len Randolph

Here in the only Chinese restaurant for 150 miles
        all of us waiting for hamburgers listen
        to the latest on John Wayne's open heart.

The one flag in this town always unfurling is the wave
        of yellow dust aging billboards into WANTED posters.

Instahomes and trailers are flung across the spring prairies
        like a new deck of cheap cards that tatter at a touch
        and the whole town's one ongoing game.

Money cuts the deck.

Wind deals.

Each night stars range like headlights from
        a 3-D freeway in some lonesome cowboy's dream.

Bedrooms glow blue till dawn.

The newborn's heart can't beat, won't beat, holds its breath
        for a new start somewhere else.

We listen to Paul Harvey gust through static as the only
        pair of goldfish in Wyoming, both male,
        circle their bright coffin sinking slowly
        toward the live Chop Suey at the bottom,
        wobbling back up like feeble dragon-kites.

The hamburgers arrive. The fries are raw.

We all wear one expression.

The look of the traveler realizing
        suddenly he is on the wrong bus out of town and doesn't care.

Gillette, Wyoming

THE LORD'S CIRCUS
As Told by the Waitress at an All-Night Diner in West Texas

One night last year, about this time, nothing but that busted hunk of neon moon out there and nothing in here but the roaches in the cups and me, there was this pack of bikers come roaring in off the road in their black leather all hungry for a good time and figuring I was it.

One wore most his own teeth strung out like a Cheshire grin across his bare chest and drooled in a fancy lace hankie when he laughed. Beer and fries was what they ordered but I knew it was trouble coming up when Hank pulled in, them trailer lights on his big rig blinking like the Lord's circus, the rumble of that warmed-up diesel muttering like lions in the dark.

Now Hank's no fool. He seen the hidden knives glitter in their eyes, the steel-toe boots dangling from the stools they spun around on, staring. He just set down grinning back and when the drooler took it in his head to stir up salt in Hank's black coffee he still grinned and there they set, bumper to bumper, while that engine muttered like a pride of lions in the dark outside.

And when they run him down name by rude name, insult by insult, he just grinned, his knuckles whiter than that cup dwarfed in his hands. They had their fun and skinned him out with words and when they let him go they howled so loud that not one noticed how he backed that flashing rig of his out, toppling the whole row of bright chained bikes like chrome dominoes and crushing every one before he drove off in the dark again, lighting up the highway with his grin.

SOMETIMES HEAVEN IS A MEAN MACHINE
for Wayne Sloan

It is like riding Death and not dying.

It shudders, snarls and roars like an iron lion,
it shines like the chromed bones of a bull.

At night its single headlight
rakes across the highway like the lowered horn
        of a charging unicorn.

It looks like Death waiting for a taker.

You take it, you ride.

All day, all night for years
while the bright arcs of your breath flex
        into curves repeating earthshapes,
                you ride, the road informing you.

You ride
your own death and you do not die.

It shines and you ride its shining.

WORKING BY THE RIVER OF LOST SOULS
for Red Bird

That's a poetic title, nonetheless true
if you take the local histories for true,
but the Animas at flood is definitely muddy
with earth washed down from upriver slopes
as I'm working out a new table of contents
for the book you're holding now, when my dog,
Oscar, growls.
        "Hey, mister, what shoe dune?"
asks a young man unsteady on his legs.
"Is that insurance papers or something?"
As we talk I can see he's thirsty for more
of the whatever's got him wobbling
and my heart sinks. He's been on the road
a long time, lost his pack and cash at
a bus stop in Boise. He's been to Detroit,
St Louis, Tulsa— "I seen it all, like the eagle
of my people" he says, then asks if I believe in
Christ, adding "I take that dude for my savior."
The river rushing in front of us is just
the color of his face. I point out a mallard
bobbing through rapids just as it takes off
then he points to three more riding easier
currents next to shore. "Some take it easy,
some go for the gusto. I like to live every
minute every day," he proclaims. "Like the
bald eagle of my people." "Well, I'm about
bald as an eagle," I offer, smiling, but not him,
he's watching the river. "You're no eagle, bro."
I don't argue. He grins. "So let's hear a poem."
And I read one about watching a baby pigeon
sitting oblivious in a bull-snake's mouth

as the snake slowly swallows and how we
can do nothing for such a one but witness
its fate. He likes it, we shake hands in
a clumsy three-part handshake that ends
clasping wrists. He asks for money for coffee
and I give him a dollar. Before he leaves
he tosses back his head and his eyes
above the broad cheekbones gleam. "Maybe
some day you'll write one about me?"

Durango, Colorado

TRUCK TALKING LATE

To His Partner

Hell no, it's not my
charming personality
—old Truck can be
three-quarters SOB
95% of the time,
stubborn as a mule
in a burning barn
the other half. I
can't ask no one
to listen. All
I can do
is talk and say
if you don't like it
stick it in your ear.
It's not my charm
has got me where I am.

And just where am I?
        Nowhere,
a shorthair trucker
getting the shaft at work
from some longhair hippy.
Now I don't take no shit,
not off nobody. But I won't
stand up to you, buddy,
and argue—what the hell's
the use
to argue? Stone
on stone, that's what.

To His Wife

Now you just goddamn shutup.
You just shut up
and hear me out.
You got no evidence
not one shred
that I been carrying on
with other women. If
I been carrying on
you got no evidence, none.

To The Waitress

Me I do not know how to act.
Truck is one obnoxious SOB.
If you don't believe me
ask my daddy.

I don't think there's
anyone on this earth
more hot tempered,
more wild, more cold
to the core than me.

And no good goddamn woman
on this God's green earth
can straighten me out.
I can be good
three months, six months,
then some wildassed turn
comes on—I'm gone.
Just some wildassed turn,
I don't know.

To Himself

I wish to hell someone
had screwed my head on
different—I was born
bad blood
in a bad time getting worse.

I got the knowledge,
I got the will power,
I got the foresight.
If I want to step back
I can see it.
I get scared.
I get scared
of consequences. I take
the bit in my mouth
and it's like a sick dog
taking a belly of grass.

I never felt a day
in my life that
anybody really cared
if Truck stayed on the road
or went on over.

HOW UNCLE LUCKY GOT THAT WAY
for Ralph E. Spurlock

How'd he get that name, you say?
I'll tell you how.
                    Our people
back in Michigan got word
how there was good to be had
over there in Jordan, Montana,
so they packed up
their women and the wagons
and set out at first thaw.

What should of took weeks
took months. Gumbo, you see.
Had to scrape the gumbo off
their wagon wheels ever few feet
or horses couldn't haul em.
Arrived early June, they did,
the blue-joint hay hand-high,
and started harvesting
soon as they had shelter.
Took a mite of a while—
didn't have no pitchforks
nor the means
to put it up.
                    Come fall, though,
they sent him on to Miles City
with the works, to trade out
for winter supplies and maybe
a barrel of whiskey spirits
to keep their own from lagging.

Well, he was gone some time,
he was, and come back
a hoopin and a hollerin
with two whisky barrels

in the wagon. Nothing more.
Them barrels wasn't sea-cured
so all the way they rolled round
and broke up and run dry.

Winter coming on, them hills afire
with warning—pretty to look at,
right painful to consider.
My daddy and the others,
they like to killed him
then and there—
lucky they needed
ever sorry pair of hands
they could find in those days.

Lucky fellah, they'd say later
when his name come up.
Lucky none
a them horses died
he'd taken off to Miles City.

Brought em back
looking like they'd gone
the full five thousand,
grazing as they had to
on what it is a horse
can graze on tied
to the hitching rail
of the Miles City saloon.
But they was alive still,
if worse the wear,
and he was some worse too,
so they didn't shoot him.

And lucky they got buffalo
enough to stretch out
through the lean months
or they'd et his ass
for Easter, sure. Lucky
for him, is what they said
all that winter. And the Lucky stuck.

JUST FOR BEING GEORGE
And this would be in memory of George Uschuk

When the doc says
"A man in
your condition
can't hope for much"
to a man
in your condition

       emphysema
       congestive heart failure
       diabetes—& now this
       spineless diagnosis
       on top of
       double pneumonia

what the hell
else is a guy
going to do

       after four years being regularly
       decorated and promoted as
       tail-gunner upsidedown over
       Italy and New Guinea both
       and then busted back
       just for being George
       then thirty years more taking flack
       from shift-bosses back
       at the Olds plant days
       and capping your homebrew nights
       for all those buddies who
       landing in the Deadman's Float
       on Lake Yesterday
       one by one bailed out on you

what else
but get pissed enough
to go home to Ella
and raise unholy Russian hell

    about that sorry-assed
    assistant SOB
    whose insult
    left you no choice

but to get well?

UPON LEARNING A FRIEND'S NAME
HAS BEEN ADDED TO THE QUILT
In Memory of Bob Mony

Foregoing, by way of burlesque, whatever may've tempted us
toward the tragic—that was your early style, the one
by which I knew you first, and best, three decades back
when we were all still undergrads, ill-defined. Red-haired,
freckled, with specs and a ready wit, you were, as friend
Tim put it, "a tad light in the loafers," yet so ferociously
intent crouched hovering over the glowing keyboard,
you electrified your friends, straight and gay alike.
Classical thunder that broke from your flashing hands
sustained the fire steady in your eyes through long nights
we all spent in the laughing haze of the *Blue Moon Tavern.*
When your shoehorn-slender friend, Joel, took to bed to
do his flirty Deborah Kerr to your carrot-topped Yul Brenner,
I remember you were mortified by your sheer delight. Then
when he left for Paris, apprentice to a master pianist,
all of us were envious. Someone's life was taking off!
We were left on the dock, waving, helplessly ourselves,
our Seven-league dreams outrun by another's actual feat.
How many years did you spend then as hired accompanist
invisible to thunderous phalanxes of beginning dancers
before your bodybuilding so bulked up that scrawny frame
I'd never have known you on the street?

                              All I knew came from Tim,
who told me, told me just today, over his blurred breakfast of
shot-gunned triple bourbons, that yesterday you died. Blurted
it out because what other way was there to say it. And so, I realized,
you'd died distant as Manhattan at an eclipse of the full moon.
And someone who'd caught your pioneering TV spot for AIDS
paid your way, just in time, for two last weeks of King's X
in exotic Hawaii—home to more endangered species
than anywhere else on earth. Gentle-hearted, wry, so rare,
you were one of the good guys, a lover of poetry, music,

and wit honed to an edge so fine a victim hardly knew
the necklace of blood at his throat was his own.
                                                    So, if
I say your life has had its own modern fairy-tale ending,
registering the grim mystery in your own droll key, I trust
you would approve. May you sleep well, brother Mony,
and by flawless music be relieved of all your dreams.

AT HANNAH'S FEAST
for Tim and Hannah Riley

Here's one for you, Tim, best friend from days we hardly knew
then would prove our youth. First, picture this: aeolian Li Po

at the feast of his last breath, translated from Wen I-To's characters
overlaid by my memories of you and your own mortal crew.

Remember your last lamb roast for Hannah, her grand spring hurrah,
how you loved to watch a young moon dance among bobbling
    waters? So,

unavoidably, there turned the poor young thing sprigged and tastily
    spitted
above hot coals where we all sat, chattering, as it hissed,

splattered and seared golden and you kept everyone
in stitches with the wicked lampoons and loopy dry asides

that could've brought an army of unBelievers to their knees
(or brought on an army of Believers, hood-headed, with torches),

serving up skewered stupidities of the left, the righteous
and the lukewarm in Gatling fashion, a Confucian hitman,

deadly prelude to a feast had the slaughter not amused us. Yes,
I write, but it's you who are true laureate of all things hapless,

armed to the gills with prickly wit, unbeaten heart, and pointy quills
loosed straight to their marks, all Dicks and Bloody Marys.

And then after the feast and after Burt's wife rose and danced
among the demolition of bones and bottles on the wet tabletop,

after the thanks belched from all quarters of the deck and dark
and the sleepy nods of infants in arms, and the stoned snarls

of couples still at odds over who'd been with whom in the can,
and the TV's neon flaring in the living room, and the cat the cat—

the cat you catapulted cart-wheeling toward the Milky Way...
then the yowling guests began to leave. Friends from work,

friends strictly from hunger, friends no one's ever seen before
with lamb ribs and silver poking out of their wife-beaters,

aging bikers with spiders webbing their bare skulls blue,
biker chicks with stretch-mark butterflies fluttering,

punks with their pierced lips, shrinks with piercing glances,
all gone. All. All but the cat, who crept back in from the night

unrepentant and unharmed, alert and curious, curling up just where
you lay your story-roaring down on folded forearms, purring.

PASSING GO

Bowlegged behind her cane
on Market Street
in late afternoon
she waits as sure
of a streetcar
as cactus is of rain,
patchwork satchel
vivid against the dark
wedge of her coat.

Mist curls at
her swollen ankles
like a lap dog
she ignores.

As the racket pauses
she hauls herself aboard,
lurches
when it starts.

*Hey lady
you didn't pay!*

She halts, spins round,
points the cane. You men,
*you're all alike—
All you want to do is fuck!*

She slips into a seat,
winks at the lady
stiffened beside her.

Whispers in her ear,
*Works every time now
don't it, dear?*

A STEP IN THE DANCE

Wind moves blindly
through the casual hair
of the hobo immobile
on the moving train
—this man
who does not move,
who gets where he's going.

SALMONDREAM
for Judith Anne Azrael

Salmon in the river blur
like dreams, then reappear
to break the surface
with disturbances healing
at the speed of light.

We watch, intent, blind
to the clouds and leaves
swimming the wind. By chance
I watch a forked twig running
at the speed of water

pass over the falls and the falls
freeze into focus: A salmon
springs from froth
solid as snow. Each scale is clear
and our universe, inverted in that eye,

shines as far and brilliant as the moon.
You are there and I am there, all of this,
caught forever in the alien lens
of an eye staring from the face
assumed by water. Seen and gone.

SLUGS AMOROUS IN THE AIR

> *"The spirit moves,*
> *Yet stays:*
>
> *...*
> *A small thing,*
> *Singing."*
> *—Theodore Roethke*

On mucous films they glide,
gracefully monstrous:

slick misbegotten whales,
halved, cast out onto land,

shrunken, left to cross forever
the shoreless sea of earth.

Indifferent to us,
these constant voyagers

detecting in each other clues
of readiness—who knows how?

They soar like gradual
eagles up a bank of tree

out onto a dark current
of limb, then dangle

from a single length
of shared umbilicus

high in clear blue
air, spinning

slowly in the globe
of their own motion,

two beings intent
upon each other

as only lovers are,
each laved by the liquid other

in body-length embrace.
Like darkly pairing tongues

or the sundered halves
of Leviathan

trying bright reunion
in their sea of air,

they hang in that whole kiss
while we look on

radiant with disgust and envious,
pitching toward awe

as from each head
organs emerge unfurling

like silk parachutes
exquisite with awareness,

each coddling its exact
other in the counterfeit

with a long careful touching,
numinous as saints,

unutterably lewd
as they merge

in a bright soft lock
joined as orchids

might join if animated
by desire, trembling

blossom against blossom,
slow pulse

matching slow pulse
as these doubly sexed

beings will do,
continuing an hour

and more,
each gross shape further

extending (from the chill
of what should be

its head) the lucent
figure of an organ

wholly sexual as angels,
male and female brilliance twinned.

And what passes
between them

in this urgent healing
sought by the never whole

passes slow as nectar
shining in the deepest

flower we know
and multiplies

into these glistening miracles
we who grow gardens

in our annoyance
never guess.

ARCTIC
        for Robert Hedin

From its polished display case
this one stares back at us,
almost contemptuous.

Dead claws hooked
in the lifelike branch,
its beak is half parted
as if to remark
on the brass
of the nameplate
where Greco-Latin nominations
encase him in another
kind of glass
to be held back by,
beheld in.
                    No wind
will alert him
of our presence.
No snapped branch
set him
soaring like a moon
among glazed clouds.
Nor will the museum's
rats tempt him
in the dark
to hunch and spread
his wings and tail and fall
silent as moonlight
upon the quick hot
frenzy in that fur.

Nor in fact could anything be said
to move him now.
This is what we learn

from him, if
we learn at all: That he
is dead, stuffed
among the mystery
of all that has been.
Is changed as we
are changed,
gazing upon him.

    Moon-eyed Owl,
    for whom the night is eyes,
    Cloud-voiced Owl,
    charged by the intelligence
    of snow to utter brilliance,
    it is you, Lightning-taloned,
    you of the Arrow-tongue,
    you alone who know to summon
    from the live red flesh that breath
    bright as dew called from grasses by the sun.

    And it is you, Whose-Feathers-Whisper,
    you of whom it is known
    that we will
    hear him
    one day, or one night,
    hear him call our name
    in a language of light
    that must illuminate us
    each in the locked museum
    of all we thought
    we knew and, having heard,
    we will rise up
    nearer to his voice
    on our unfathomable wings
    to ask who he was calling for, who? Who?

ABOVE BLACKHAWK WHERE AIR GETS THIN
for Val

Out hiking a mud-rutted road
above Black Hawk, pines dark
on each side, my friend and I
stopped chatting when a squeak
took shape before us—chipmunk
with a ferret like an elongated
shadow hot on its heels
barely fifty feet ahead. So low
to the ground they ran
those ruts were trenches good
enough, almost, to hide in.
The chipmunk, exhausted,
squatted panting, eyes wide,
ignoring us, head fatally
raised. Three times
its length, the ferret
almost casually loped up
behind it, grabbed it by
the back of the neck. No
drama at all. The chipmunk
gave it up, scarcely even
trying to escape as ferret
simply ran back off into
thin pines with its meal. We
were stunned not by the fight
that never happened, but by
the gentlemen's agreement kept
so civil we felt like beasts.

BLUE LAKE DREAM

1.
I float upon a lake, suspended
In my simple boat of skin.

All above me is the azure
Blazing of the inner bowl.

Below and all around
Extends the mirror, tense and blue.

I am floating on my back,
Arms spread, legs parallel, eyes wide.

2.
I am drawn swirling upward
By the vacuum of the dome,

Rushing downward by the massive depths:
Slowly on the surface I revolve.

All around the great blue
Mountains of the shore

Ring me with increasing force,
Pull with power absolute

And absolutely countered
By the magnet of my heart.

Between explosion outward
And collapse within

I am witness
To the awe of stasis,

I, who am Lodestone,
I, Brain,

I, inner sun
Utterly ablaze in the ark of the Skull.

3.
Floating on my back I am turning
As Earth turns—flung out from the center,

Drawn in by the core—,
Arms spread, eyes wide.

Eyes gone blind as stone.
Eyes made clear as diamond.

4.
In my skull grows
A light
Brighter than all the fire
Round Salamander's hull

Who sets forth through the wavering of flames
Who will not dwell in fire

Who shall pass through.

FOR THE WOLF AT MY DOOR
A Sort of Apology

While I type
    in she trots
        out of open daylight,

a hundred pounds of girl wolf,
    her laser-gaze golden,
        her soft ears half cocked.

When I lean down
    to rub muzzles with her,
        sandgrains on her chin

give her away:
    She's been
        in the garden again,

devotedly burying bones
    or digging them up,
        and now she's smuggled

into the study
    with all its musty books
        the stuff of fields and forests,

the odor of
    earth freshly stirred,
        in a word

fertile ground!
    Bless you,
        Lulu Garou,

you've done the work
    cut out for you.
        Now let me do mine.

The cover art for this book is "White Boots"
© 1988 James G. Davis.
The text of the book is typeset in 10-point Minion.
The book was designed by Lesley Landis Designs
and printed by Central Plains Book Manufacturing.